ECD

INDIA · SINGAPORE · MALAYSIA

Notion Press

No.8, 3rd Cross Street,
CIT Colony, Mylapore,
Chennai, Tamil Nadu – 600004

First Published by Notion Press 2020
Copyright © Priyanka Bedi 2020
All Rights Reserved.

ISBN 978-1-64892-684-6

ECDYSIS
SHEDDING OLD SKIN

PRIYANKA BEDI

INDIA · SINGAPORE · MALAYSIA

INDICACADEMY

INDIC PLEDGE

—◆◆—

- *I celebrate our civilisational identity, continuity & legacy in thought, word and deed.*

- *I believe our indigenous thought has solutions for the global challenges of health, happiness, peace and sustainability.*

- *I shall seek to preserve, protect and promote this heritage and in doing so,*
  - *discover, nurture and harness my potential,*
  - *connect, cooperate and collaborate with fellow seekers,*
  - *advance diversity and inclusivity in the society.*

ABOUT INDIC ACADEMY

—◆◆—

Indic Academy is a non-traditional 'university' for traditional knowledge. We seek to bring about a global renaissance based on Indic civilizational and indigenous thought. We are pursuing a multidimensional strategy across time, space and cause by establishing centers of excellence, transforming intellectuals and building an ecosystem.

Indic Academy is pleased to support this book.

I hope you find the lost pieces of yourself when you read this book.
I hope it heals your heart the way writing heals mine.

Give me all the pain you carry in your heart
I'll use it to grow happiness within me

For what I know
Setting your heart free from the hurt
Will be my redemption

to my family of four

write your heart out on the journal pages inside as you read Ecdysis and share your thoughts with me on Instagram @the.priyanka.bedi

she was beautiful
she was breathtaking
but she was quiet
long enough to kill my heart
with every breath i took
her silence made my demons
ache in awe
a heavenly catastrophe

i give and give
without expecting
anything in return
i love like my mother does

my love is wild
your city arms can't handle it

and for some reason i know
i will never fall in love with you
not because you're unlovable
but my heart is too fragile
for your clumsy hands
handle with care

my heart is still a virgin
it feels as if all this while
men found a way inside me
but never made it to my heart

my heart is still a virgin
maybe because it's never been loved

you're so afraid
of not being loved
the right way
that you decide
rather overfill someone's heart with it
than let someone leave yours half empty
i wonder
how beautiful yet tragic
that feeling must be?

unexpressed love is nothing
but flowers
that never bloomed

i am afraid to write about you
i feel my words will fall short
before i even start describing you
my rhymes won't be sweet enough
to describe the honey in your words
my poems won't be good enough
to explain what your touch does to me
but even more than that
i am afraid that if i write about you
i will never be able to stop

and you, my darling
were turning the heartbreak in my poetry
into healing
how could i not believe
that i was in love
again

For years, I've been familiar with all the wrong
ways to define love. I've let all the wrong people in
and thought that maybe that was what I really
deserved—maybe that was what love was.

But now, here you're lying with me, looking at the
ceiling. We're inches away from touching each other.
I expect you to make a move, kiss me, get on top or
hold my hand at the least. But you don't do anything.
You just lie with me and smile. You talk.

I'm not used to talking. I'm used to being dominated,
controlled. I'm used to physical intimacy but this
emotional connection that you're trying to build,
it's beyond my understanding.

You're too good to be true. It makes my heart ache.
Something inside me dies because all these years, I've been
searching for love in all the wrong places. I've given my
fragile heart in the hands of those who had no intention
of keeping it. But now, here you're holding it like it's all
that matters in the world. You're trying to protect it. You're
trying to love it and it feels too good to be true.

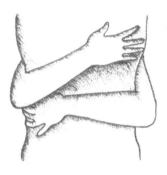

my soul found solace in your words
i wonder what magic
wearing your arms around me would do?

tangle your hands with mine
some knots are better left tied

you leave me every night
with hope for tomorrow
you're the sun
my nights wait for

will you stay with me
even when i push you away?
will you hold me in your arms
when i can't touch myself?
will you walk me to the end
when i can't even crawl?
will you hold onto us
when i have given up?
will you love us both
when i can't love either of us?

and some nights i wonder
how it feels
to be a part of something
so pure
so beautiful
so intimate

i wonder how it feels
to be a part of my poetry
write about me, can you?

you left too soon
before i could
embrace your touch

but

you stayed long enough
for me to remember
how your touch felt

and then there are people
like you
who last
just for a fraction of second
but still make it to my poems

the time for which
a flower blooms
does not validate
its beauty

similarly

the time for which
our relationship lasts
does not validate
our love

and there shall be a sky
worth everything, after us
but it won't shine the same
with our absence underneath

you made sure
that i picked your habits
so when you leave
don't just take away
the things that belong to you
take me with you too
for what i know
i have got traces of you
left within me

i know that loving you is going to hurt
the question is, are you worth it?

you're a poem
the one which personifies love
you're an extract
the one which has all the right words
you're a narration
the one which describes all the beauty of this world
you're a play
the one which has all the right kind of characters
but it doesn't matter how beautiful my eyes picture you
because at the end
you belong to a different book
and you're not mine to read

the only mistake i ever made
was to fall for you
in ways i shouldn't have, best friend

maybe you weren't supposed to be the one
who would hold me tight on winter nights
but the thought that would bother my mind
when i am alone on a flight

maybe you weren't supposed to be the one
who would share with me, my home
but the one who would make me cry less often
as i grew old

maybe you weren't supposed to be the one
i would get my wedding ring from
but the one whose memories for a moment
would take away all my warmth
first love

maybe in some parallel universe
we'll meet, again
we'll fall in love, again
and maybe this time
you'll stay
possibilities

but i can never get all of you at once
not in this lifetime
so i will wait for my body to burn
i will wait for the day when i step into heaven
because maybe not when i am alive
but i will be with you in my afterlife

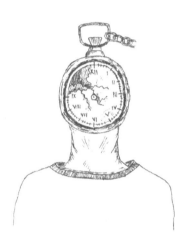

i will have you
in some other time zone
for now you're not mine
and that is it

oh love, you were the five-star wine
while i was the countryside beer
you were the conditioned air of hotel rooms
and i was the early morning breeze

but still

we gave a shot at us
and just like oil and water
we were always together
yet so far

you can pack your things
keep them at the doorstep
leave before its dawn
i won't stop you, i promise

but tonight?
stay

just stay with me
i need you

i wonder if i am falling for you
or is it just one of those nights when
you're the closest thing i have to him

we weren't in love
we were in need
the need to feel
a little less broken
a little less alone
the need to feel loved
even if it's for one night
a moment of vulnerability

tonight, when i kiss you
remember
it's just our bodies
that are tangled
my soul is still
connected to his
superficial attachments

we're not together
we're tangled
it's not the same

we may never be lovers
but you'll always be the one
who restored my faith in love
and i will be forever thankful for that

your eyes don't even blink
when you say you love me
they pierce right through mine
daring me to question your honesty
i am afraid
even your eyes are familiar
to the art of lying

you only love me when you need me
that's why you're like water to me
and i am just a glass of wine to you

you come to love me
when my thorns have broken
and buds flowered
you love me when it's easy

how tragic it is, my love
we could have been
the most beautiful things together

early morning dew on the leaves
cold breeze on a sunny day
the bright colours of a rainbow
tender waves on the sea-shore
most beautiful sunflowers of the garden
two stars shining alone in the night sky

yet we chose to be nothing
but the worst of us

we weren't ready when we fell in love
too young to realise how precious and beautiful
this relationship was
so we did what people do to precious things
we ruined it

but it's easy for you to say
i am afraid of commitments
destiny wants something else
maybe we are not meant to be

rather than accepting
you don't want to try even
so you put the blame on something
i can't question

you blame fate
for all the wrongs
you do

you might blame destiny
for what happened to us
but darling
you and i
we both know
you chose this for us
you did this to us

he thinks love is an emotion
which makes people weak
maybe that is why
he hates me
convincing

you're quite a cigarette, they say
unsettling at first
weirdly familiar with every puff
a little rough
bitter taste
hallucinating smoke rings
a cold soul's ashes
keeping me warm
amidst this chaotic mess
what is it about you
reason of my end
yet everything i need
to stay awake

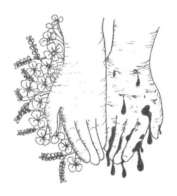

you make me long for your love
when you're done giving me the hate
you disappear at night
just to make me wait for the day

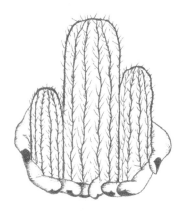

you didn't just come to pluck my flowers and leave me bare
you came with the intention to tear each petal apart
for i would feel the loss of each one of them
for you would see me bleed for each one of them

you didn't just come to stab me all at once
you came with the intention to peal off every inch of my skin
love, a slow death

some days i think you are just a tired soul
trying to project its pain in me
maybe because you've been holding up all your emotions
for what i know it's been ages
since you opened the door for healing
because they've always told you
hide it, don't show
you're a man

whatever may be the reason
i don't know and i don't care
because today i am paying
for what they did to you
toxic masculinity

you keep me full
just to be the one who makes me starve
you heal my skin
so you're the one who puts the scars
but even my scars don't please you
it's the screams
that make you smirk
you don't want to lock me in the dark
you want to see me beg for the light
making sure to quench my thirst
only after you've seen me
long for the very last drop
there's nothing human about you

you're what happens
when insanity and possession
come dressing as love

i could feel the blood travelling in every vein of my body
while i took long breaths to release the tension
my fists clenched so tight
as my nails dug deeper in the skin of my palms
my eyes turned red as wine
too satanic to look at
i cupped my body
bringing my knees close to my chest
my hands unconsciously searched for things to break
and grabbed the hold of roots of my hair
breaking a couple strands
as i felt no pain
i punished myself
for the crimes you did
anger

i pour my soul in a kettle
and serve it you like bed time tea
i lay my body on the table
and become your greatest feast
i pierce my lips with knife
and satisfy your sweet tooth
with the honey it bleeds
i perish my soul
to fulfil your needs
i kill myself a little
every time you breathe

but i won't run away or hide
i am the toxic type
i crave the sensation of being alive
and it lies in the pain you inflict

so when you utter those words
i don't dodge them this time
i stand still letting them prick
tearing me into pieces
i can't recognise

i listen, i listen, i listen
letting my ears bleed
crying my eyes out
till they run out dry
and when there's nothing left
for you to destroy
i stand still

only this time
i listen, i listen, i listen
and i don't feel a thing

it doesn't hurt
it gives me chills
like a cold winter midnight
or a morgue full of death bodies
the words you say

remember how you once accidentally cut my veins open?
they bled poetry
and now i let strangers walking by
pierce deeper into that wound
just to see
what more beauty they can bleed

i write my misery and they clap
my pain is their fascination
and i intend to keep them fascinated
as long as i shall feel
i will keep writing

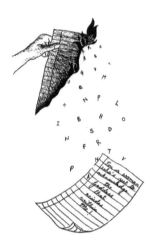

you might burn the pages
i write my poetry on
they will still scream the words
from the ashes and beyond
making their presence felt

My heart has been cold for too long now. The sense of feeling anything is long forgotten. I've been looking for someone, who can bring it to life again. Break down the walls I've built and stay in there. I'm not asking for love. I'm not asking for care either. All I wish for is a sensation, something I can feel. Just an emotion to remind me that I'm still alive. This heart of mine isn't dead, as I think of it.

Come in, the door's open.
Make a home out of it, take care of it or shatter it if you want.
A godsend or a catastrophe, be anything.
Just get me out of the numbness that surrounds my heart.
dead inside

for years, i bottled up my emotions
without realising when they formed an ocean
and today, this ocean is calling on me
demanding every part of me
to drown in it

this ocean is the justice my soul needs
for all the wrongs i did to it
trying to do right by others

It is as if the Satan on my shoulder waits through the entire show of fearlessness I try to put up. He sits patiently, watching me fool my mind and smiles at the little games I try to play. He waits and waits and waits and then in that one rare moment of vulnerability, he catches me. He catches me off guard and pulls me in the riddles of denial and self-loathing.

It's funny yet tragic, how I'm both.

the hunter and the prey

i have left pieces of mine
in the poetry I plant on pages
i have let the darkest side of my heart
shine in the rhymes I write
i have let my wounds bleed
and colour the poems scarlet red
because that is how I write
and you, my love
read it all, every day
and yet, yet
you don't understand me
but you claim to love me?

you expect me to understand your silence
but you don't even understand
the crystal clear words I say
and you say you love me

i showed you my love like the seven shades of rainbow
but never let my expectations fall on you like the rain
and you like a fool never bothered to think
how do these rainbows show up
in places it never rains?

you don't ask for my forgiveness
you demand it
you don't care if you deserve it
all you know is that you need it
there is an ocean of difference between the two

i stole the love
i had for myself
just to keep you satisfied
i cheated on me
just to do right by you
i let my heart crumble
just to keep yours intact
how was any of this
unfair to you?
false allegations

even at your worst
i tried to find something
to hold on to and not leave
yet you dared to question my love

my physics professor once told me
even when i am waving a finger in air
i am disturbing the balance of the universe
wonder what destruction your absence
would have caused in mine?

and as for the world
it slowed down
and fell silent
while the storm inside me
had just begun

you didn't just break my heart
you made it incapable of loving someone ever again

i was wandering in the desert of loneliness
and you appeared like an oasis to me
but just like water, your love for me dried out
and now all i have are these mirages
which remind me of you

i wonder if your heart aches
remembering the love i gave you
like mine does
remembering the pain you gave me

it's easy to tell myself that i cared
more than i should have
than accepting the fact that
you didn't care at all

I miss you I

no matter how hard i try to forget you
my words always find their way back to you

your claws were embedded way too deep in me
it's impossible for me to just ignore the scars now

but I'm so afraid
so afraid to let anyone in
ever again

because if i do
it would mean
letting them see the mess you left
letting them make their own space in the chaos you created
letting them disturb the last of what's left of you
it would mean
giving up the last of you

and i am not ready to let you go
not now, not ever

my heart has been numb
for way too long now
you were the last sensation it felt

and after you
no loss was worth grieving
you were and always will be
my greatest loss

you were my most tragic story
you will be my most beautiful poetry
the more i bleed
the more my words shine
wounds, poetry, me

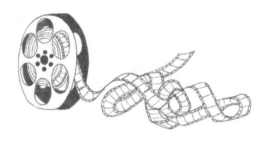

and maybe i am just replaying our story
over and over again
processing every possible version in my head
trying to figure out that one time
that one perfect series of moments
in which we last

but we don't
not even once

every version of our story falls apart
sometimes a little sooner
sometimes a little later
no matter what changes i make
we just don't last

maybe it would've hurt less
if i would've known
what you were looking for
was a rental apartment
and not a home

for i know
i wouldn't have hung pictures of you
or planted those flowers in your name
just to see you move out someday

Ecdysis

maybe you were the butterfly
and my love felt nothing
but a cage holding you back

i was trying to build you a home
on the surface
but you belonged in the sky

maybe that is why
even when my touch was filled
with nothing but love
it felt like a prison to you

maybe if i had sensed the fear
as your wings fluttered
maybe if i had let you go
you would still be mine

but how do i let go of someone
who was never mine?
how do i move on
from something
that never existed?

i don't regret
falling for you
however
i do regret believing
that you fell for me too

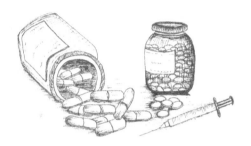

what brand of pain
did you inject me with?
even my poetry is failing
as an antidote this time

and i am still hoping for it to be a bad dream
the way you looked at her
the way your eyes shone saying her name

i am still hoping for it to be a bad dream
and i am still waiting for you to wake me up from it

my fingers trembled with agony
my lips parted and became dry
i could trace the patterns on them
my body radiated heat
even though i had just one layer of sweater on
i was sweating
i felt a pit in my stomach
while the bile reached my throat
giving me a burning sensation
making me unable to utter a word even
my eyes filled with tears—
tears that had no right to travel down my burning cheeks
the pit in my stomach deepened with every moment that passed
my heart was pounding and take my word on this
if it wasn't for my ribs
it would've jumped right out of my chest
that's what losing you to someone felt like
when you weren't even mine
jealousy

your words shattered my heart
more than your actions ever could
for what i know
i blinded my eyes with your love
but i couldn't *un-hear* what you said

but what if you're not there
what if you weren't ever there?
what if all i was holding on to was an image of you
what if you're nothing but a painting i painted in my head
what if you're nothing like i see you
what if the person in my head and the person you're
are two different people?
what if the person i love doesn't exist?
what if all of this has always been just in my head?

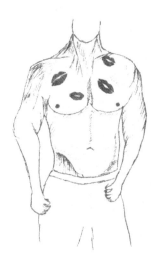

i drew petals on your chest
just to see you paint them in red
with her lipstick

you sucked out the good in me
and complained about what was left
the evil

you walked away and left words behind
i weaved
our memories
your lost love
my pain
everything into poetry

but now all of this is fading away
and so is my poetry

come back
love me, again
hurt me, again
i can't write

you filled my veins with hate
the blood that knew nothing
but poetry
is black—like venom
and calling out your name
come back

it's a pity that i am still writing about you
while you're playing the lead in someone else's book

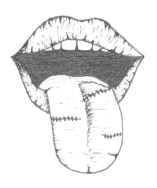

i am over you
i say
as i write another poem
in your name
i lie

and i will keep writing about you
until i run out of words
because only when my pages are overfilled
with poetry written about you
my heart will be free from the hopes
i am holding on to
and i will let you go

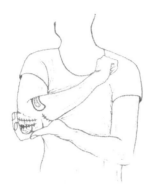

you were the thorn
that clung to my skin
longer than it should've
i was afraid to take you out
thinking
what if it hurts?
what if i bleed?
and the wound never heals
denial

i took a step back and looked at you
my heart crumbled at the sight of your apologetic face
but as the forgiveness was about to settle in
a storm of rage and disgust raided my heart
i couldn't forgive you with a still-hurting heart

Priyanka Bedi

if loving someone fills your heart with warmth
then why does it feel cold when it breaks?
if loving someone fills your heart with joy
then why does it bleed pain when it breaks?

and i wonder
how can someone break the heart
they once called their home?

we didn't break at once
we drifted apart
so slow that it didn't exactly hurt

we were too blind
to see the increasing distance
or perhaps we didn't want to

for what we know
it was too late to make up
for the things we did
words we said
apologies we didn't confess

so we moved along with it
trying to ignore
what our hearts knew
but eyes denied to see

until it was too late
to look back and see
if there was anything left at all
that we could hold onto

but now with everything ending
we realise that
we didn't wake up one day
and give up on each other
we grew out of the love
that held us together

we didn't give up on love
we just couldn't keep it alive
or maybe we just let it die

like a jar of honey we broke
flowing away like two waves
so slow, so beautiful
heavenly tragedy

dear someone better
you're so different from the rest
so much better in all the ways i know you
yet when i look at you
it all comes down to the same thing—
you're everything better
but just not him
so my heart doesn't want you

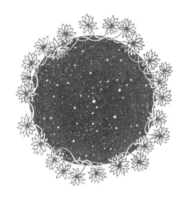

you were empty
a flower without nectar
honey without taste
a book without poetry

appealing to eyes
but no comfort to the soul
it was foolish of me
to expect anything
out of you
beautiful void

Yes, you made me so happy that, for a fraction of a second,
I forgot how it felt to be sad. You had that magic in your
words and charisma in your eyes. You were everything a
hurting heart needed—everything that I needed.

But then, I took a step back and looked at you again, with
eyes that looked past the needs—the eyes that looked at
reality—and it hit me.

I was willing to put everything I had at stake just to feel
that fraction of happiness you gave me. I couldn't do it
anymore. I couldn't give in all of me while I received nothing
but a fraction of you.

I knew leaving you was going to hurt my heart
a lot more than it already did.
But I also knew what you had to offer,
was not even near to what I deserved.

A part of me still craves your attention. I still feel this urge
to touch your skin and wander in your eyes. I miss how you
smelled, the cologne you wore, everything about you still
drives me crazy. It's like a stain on my heart, which refuses
to fade away no matter how hard I try.

But it doesn't mean that I'll let you in, ever again.
I've had my share of suffering and happiness with you.

I'm happy where I am and I won't deny the fact that
somewhere, I still care, I still love you. But the bruise you left
while leaving is darker than the colour of your love. I can't
let myself get hurt again, not anymore.

I'd rather get lost in the dark
than find my way back to you

I'd rather die drinking the unknown waters
than taste your lips ever again

I'd rather accept my doom
than live another moment of my life with you

I'd rather let my heart crumble
missing you
than let you have it back
just to see you
break it again

but it was about time when i realised
that you were taking more place
than you were supposed to

remembering you wasn't healing me
it was destroying me
all over again

i didn't stop loving you
i just learned to love myself more

the next person i love
deserves all of me
so i am taking from you
what belongs to me
my heart

but you don't feel like home anymore
your smell does not turn me on like it used to
your voice is pleasant to hear but so is of a stranger
your eyes do talk to me but i don't remember the language
it's like you're the leftover cup of coffee from last night
still a little warm when i touch
but not strong enough for a sip

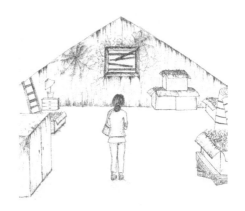

you know the house you once called home
the one you had to leave for moving on to something better
the house you have no feelings attached to
but just a sense of familiarity
that's what your arms are to me
not homely, just familiar

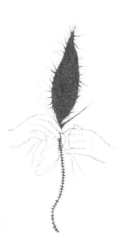

your apology means nothing now
my wounds healed waiting for you

you love going back and forth
without realising what it does to me
every time you leave
a part of me dies
but there's a part of me
that learns to live without you
which is why i know

this time when you'll shut me off
there won't be anything left in me
that your absence can kill

this time when you abandon me
the last of what's left within me
will learn to live without you

so this time when you come crawling back
i won't need you anymore

you come to water me
when i have bloomed
you come to save me
when i have escaped
you come to love me
when i have learned to love myself
you always come
a little late

so this time when you knock
i am going to keep my doors closed
i don't need you now
leave

if you can't love me for who i am
i don't want you

yes i love you and I'd take a bullet in my heart to prove that
but if you ever ask me to choose
between my self-respect and my love
i won't let love win this war, ever

if letting my heart perish
is what it takes
to make you stay
I'd rather let you go

you tricked me into believing that
my poetry existed because you did
you made me think that
my poetry needed you
i needed you
but guess what?
we don't

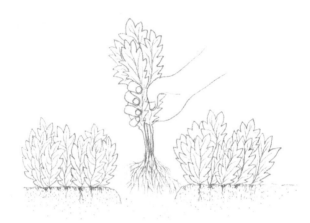

i was brave enough to love you, with all my heart
i am brave enough to leave you, with all my will

you thought your love
defined who i am
completed me as a person
and was everything i had
or needed

but honey
your love
meant so many things to me
but it wasn't my everything

even before i had you
i had me
and that's all
i will ever need

Ecdysis
————⊰⊱————

the places you weep in
grow into flowers

losing you was a road
that led me to myself

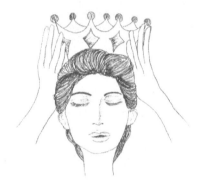

i am a woman
who's yet to acknowledge
the goddess that resides within me

the love that made you feel choked
is the one you'll crave the most
when i am not around anymore
because my love was like heroine to your heart
the one you left for some roadside beer

i could have been lying in your arms right now
but you chose a different path
and now here i am
on my way to kiss my dreams
no one's more grateful than me
about the fact that
you were a fool to let me go

i won't settle
for your piece of sky
when i know
i am worth the
galaxies

i am unapologetic for
the words I write
the love i give
the things i feel
the scars i wear
i am unapologetic
for what makes me

me

I don't think that you're ever really ready for sharing someone's love. I think you just let it come knocking on your door and as much as you don't want to let it in, you can't stop it either. So you just let it make room for itself while you hold on to your space, so tight that it physically hurts and eventually, with time, you learn to adjust.
You learn to make room.
two-bedroom heart

.

and on days
i needed to feel loved
the most
my loved ones
didn't love me
at all

and the sad part is that
you could be surrounded by people
who claim to love you
care about you
and yet
you could feel alone
loneliness hits in a crowd too

and sometimes
sadness doesn't come in waves
but a ground-shaking earthquake
and it's only after
it has done half the damage
you feel its existence

I think it is sad how we think of the ending of a relationship before it even begins. How we believe that thinking of the worst possible scenario and preparing ourselves for it will make any pain or hardship to come less hurting than it is.

how we deliberately put ourselves through hell
so that anything less feels like heaven

must you hold on to everything
like it's going to leave?
must you choke everything
before it even begins to breathe?

It's hard. it's hard to let go of connections that go back
to years of togetherness and love but when your ties with
someone start feeling toxic, you need to set yourself free
before they consume all of you.

Choosing your happiness and peace doesn't make you a bad
person. Letting go of the rose sticks when all they do is make
you bleed doesn't make you a bad person.

and sometimes people don't last
for as long as you wish them to
but that's okay
as long as you're fortunate enough
to hold on to what they leave behind
some happy moments for you to cherish
some bitter lessons for you to learn

your need for loyalty from the person you love
is not your possessiveness
don't let them take that right away from you
by labelling it something else

The thing about insecure people is that they aren't too possessive about you. They're the people who've felt the pain of being replaced too often. They've experienced how easily priorities can change for people around them. They aren't paranoid, they're just afraid of you 'losing interest' in them.

But they are the same people who will go to the edge to make you smile and prove themselves worthy of your love. They'll try to be a better person for you, every day, every moment. They'll help you grow into a better person. They're the ones who will love you unconditionally, with everything they have.

So next time you find someone who feels insecure about you, make sure you remind them that they're loved and they're enough the way they are.

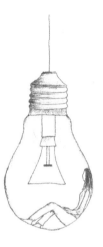

but how can you love someone
if you own a heart
that has never loved itself
i wonder

you think
loving someone is supposed to
consume you
redefine you
complete you

but, my love
something that takes your identity away from you
something that makes you think of yourself
as anything less than a complete beautiful soul
is not love
it never can be
it never will be

if all it does
is hurt you all the time
don't fear walking away

what worth is a love
which makes you sleep
with a heart that's hurt
what worth is a love
which makes you wake up
with dried tears in your eyes
love heals what's wounded

some people are like sand in your hands
the harder you try to make them stay
the more they slip out and leave
you can't build a connection based on force

you think
burning the pages on which you wrote poetry about him
plucking the flowers you planted in his name
throwing the jars of honey he tasted
cutting off everything that reminds you of him
will ease the pain you feel
and maybe bring you peace

but my baby, you and i, we both know
it was never about these material things
it was your heart that started beating for him
and you don't throw away your heart
just because someone else couldn't keep it

for you to move on
you don't have to hate him
hating him
will never fill
the hole in your heart

and with some people
it won't be easy to decide
whether to love them and stay
or to love them and let go

sometimes it's not the person that we miss
sometimes it's just the memories

don't confuse your nostalgia with love
move on with your life
you deserve happiness

do you really seek their love?
or do you just want them
to acknowledge your presence?
a need for attention, not love

the thing about love is that
you may never get it
from the places you want it to come
so while you still have the chance
appreciate the places where it already exists

the most toxic thing we do to ourselves
and the people around us
is compare our pain

we're all suffering in one way or the other
we all seek healing, equally

the way you think is the kind of energy
you give to your surroundings
and somehow, that energy always finds its way back to you
careful with the thoughts

you might be dead tomorrow
but you've a heartbeat today
and that is all you will ever need
just today

sometimes it's okay to lose sight of things
it's okay to feel lost
you don't have to figure out everything yet
you've a lifetime to do that

you don't get to decide if someone's feelings
fall under your books of righteousness or not
not everyone's heart functions the way yours does
it's okay to feel

we're all lost and trying to find pieces of
ourselves in other people

and sometimes we need someone else to believe in us
before we can believe in ourselves and that's okay

we all heal, eventually
at our own pace and that's okay

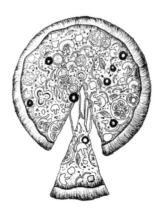

just because someone makes you happy
10 out of those 100 times
don't miss out the 90 times they hurt you
some people damage you more
than they repair you in return
know the difference

don't let the wounds
your past gave you
bleed on your present
and stain your future
let it go

i am forgiving those
who have done me bad
for what i know
i am setting us free
from the weight i carry in my heart
and the guilt you carry along
forgiveness, for you and me

just because you bloom different
does not mean that
you're any less beautiful
than the other flowers of this garden
our differences make us authentic

And you know, sometimes you're going to expect
from people, what you're willing to give them. But what
you can give to someone might be different from
what they've to offer. Your utmost level of effort
may not be the same as theirs. But it doesn't mean
that they're trying any less. They're putting in all of
what they have, it's just not the same as you. Understand
that. It makes relationships a lot less complicated.
everyone loves differently

but how do i
compare my growth
to someone else's
when i know
we're two different flowers
nurturing in different soils
blooming in our own season
spreading two different fragrances
we grow different

This is just to remind you that you will never need someone's approval to be yourself. You are enough and you're whole in yourself. Someone's presence or absence does not define your worth. Do what makes you happy. Change what you want to change about yourself. Don't let the world tell you who you are and what you are supposed to be.

i have been reaching out to corpses
hoping they'll chant
some melody in my ears
healing my heart

i searched for a saviour
in everyone around me
when all this while
it was no one but me
i am my own happy place

maybe it's not about before
or after you've been hurt
maybe it's all about the time
you heal yourself
and become something
you never knew you were
phoenix

Dear reader

I was in a really bad place when I wrote some of the poems you just read. I get it if you ever feel like you're in one place and the whole world is existing in a completely different space. I understand how difficult it can be to just get through the day sometimes because every moment just feels heavier than the last one. But you know, as much as you right now believe that this is how you're going to feel for the rest of your life or this overwhelming feeling won't ever leave your body, it's not true. Healing takes time, it's slow and tender. It will allow you, make you feel every ounce of pain and then slowly pull you out of it.

I don't want to tell you to just hang in there because I have met enough people in my life to know one fact for sure, there's a warrior, a light in all of us and no matter how much darkness corners you, that light won't ever leave you. You are not alone in this. Whatever way you're feeling, I get it, I understand and trust me, I'm there with you, your loved ones are there with you. Just breathe, it is okay and even if it isn't, it will be. Everything will work out, you'll be happy. Universe is looking out for you, sending so much love and light on your way. Till then I am here for you, through your ecdysis, always.

with love
Priyanka

Vishesh, thank you for making me do this.
Karan, thank you for this beautiful name – Ecdysis.
Kalyani, thank you for the amazing illustrations.
Shamsheer, thank you for the beautiful journal page.

To anyone who has been there for me, through my ecdysis, thank you.
A part of this exists because of you.

CPSIA information can be obtained
at www.ICGtesting.com
Printed in the USA
BVHW031049081020
590608BV00001B/136

9 781648 926846